HOW DO WE KNOW
ENERGY EXISTS?

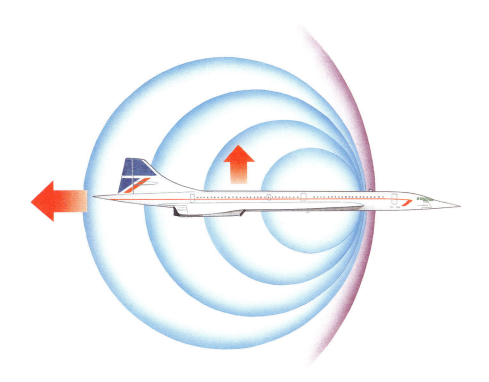

TERRY JENNINGS

RAINTREE
Steck-Vaughn
PUBLISHERS
The Steck-Vaughn Company

Austin, Texas

© Copyright 1995, text, Steck-Vaughn Company

All rights reserved. No part of this book may be reproduced or utilized in any form or by any means, electronic or mechanical, including photocopying, recording, or by any information storage and retrieval system, without permission in writing from the Publisher. Inquiries should be addressed to: Copyright Permissions, Steck-Vaughn Company, P.O. Box 26015, Austin, TX 78755

Published by Raintree Steck-Vaughn Publishers, an imprint of Steck-Vaughn Company

Commissioning Editor: Thomas Keegan
Designer: Hammond Hammond
Editor: Kate Scarborough, Maurice J. Sabean
Illustrators: Craig Austin and Alex Pang

Library of Congress Cataloging-in-Publication Data

Jennings, Terry J.
    Energy exists? / Terry Jennings.
      p. cm. — (How do we know)
    Includes index.
    ISBN 0–8114–3881–3
    1. Force and energy—Juvenile literature. 2. Power (Mechanics)—Juvenile literature. 3. Power resources—Juvenile literature. [1. Force and energy. 2. Power (Mechanics) 3. Power resources.] I. Title. II. Titie: How do we know energy exists? III. Series.
QC73.4.J46   1995
531'.6—dc20   94–20027
                                                            CIP
                                                             AC

Printed and bound in Hong Kong

1 2 3 4 5 6 7 8 9 0 HK 99 98 97 96 95 94

The words in boldface type are explained in the glossary.

Contents

HOW DO WE KNOW

Energy Exists?	4
There Are Different Types of Energy?	6
Where Energy Comes From?	8
How to Use Energy?	10
How to Store Energy?	12
What Slows Things Down?	14
Where Energy Goes?	16
Sound Is Energy?	18
Light Is Energy?	20
Food Stores Energy?	22
Prehistoric Trees Provide Today's Energy?	24
Wind and Rain Can Make Electricity?	26
Electricity Gives Us Light and Heat?	28
How Energy Gets into a Battery?	30
How to Imitate the Sun?	32
What's the Attraction?	34
How Engines Work?	36
How to Make Transportation Energy Efficient?	38
Glossary	40
Index	41

HOW DO WE KNOW

Energy Exists?

If you've got no "energy," you're either tired, ill, or just plain lazy! What does this tell us about energy? That to get moving, you must have it. However, the term *energy* doesn't just apply to people.

To a scientist, "energy" has a special meaning. However, until about 200 years ago, the scientific word *energy* had not been invented. It was first used in the 19th century, when scientists were studying the power produced by steam engines and electric motors. The word comes from the ancient Greek language and means "in work." Today scientists think of energy simply as "that which makes change happen." Scientists find out how energy can be stored and how it can be moved. They carry out experiments to show what energy does, and they compare the effects of different kinds of energy.

Without energy, plants and animals, including humans, would not be able to live, move, or grow, and machines would not be able to work. We need energy to provide us with heat and light, to entertain ourselves, and to move us from place to place.

Playing ball
When you are playing ball you are using energy. The harder you play, the more energy you use. This energy comes from the food you eat. If you kick the ball, the ball gains energy. The harder you kick it, the more energy the ball has. That energy comes from the food your muscles are using up.

Running
Whenever we move, we use energy. That energy comes from the food we eat. Running and jumping require a lot of energy. However, we also use energy when we eat, breathe, read a book, or watch television. Even when we are asleep, our bodies are using energy.

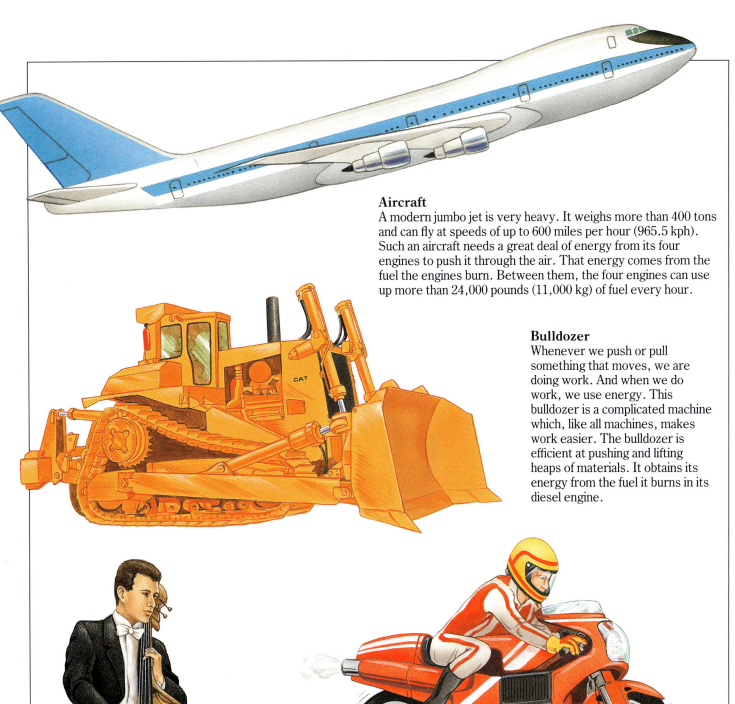

Aircraft
A modern jumbo jet is very heavy. It weighs more than 400 tons and can fly at speeds of up to 600 miles per hour (965.5 kph). Such an aircraft needs a great deal of energy from its four engines to push it through the air. That energy comes from the fuel the engines burn. Between them, the four engines can use up more than 24,000 pounds (11,000 kg) of fuel every hour.

Bulldozer
Whenever we push or pull something that moves, we are doing work. And when we do work, we use energy. This bulldozer is a complicated machine which, like all machines, makes work easier. The bulldozer is efficient at pushing and lifting heaps of materials. It obtains its energy from the fuel it burns in its diesel engine.

Musical instruments
Sound is a form of energy. The rich sounds that come from the double bass are produced by its four strings. The energy to make the strings vibrate and produce sounds comes from the muscles of the musician, who plucks the strings.

A motorcyclist
A motorcycle is another form of powered transportation. Its energy comes from the fuel it burns in its engine. Quite a lot of human muscle power is also needed to ride a motorcycle. The machine has to be steered, controlled, and kept upright with the help of the rider's muscles.

HOW DO WE KNOW

There Are Different Types of Energy?

When a light goes on, when you walk down the street, when you listen to music, when anything happens, energy is involved. But lighting a room and playing music involve two different forms of energy. In fact energy exists in many different forms, and each can do different kinds of work.

The sun is the source of most energy on Earth. People have found ways to convert its energy. They have invented machines that make work easier or that provide us with entertainment and pleasure.

For example, people have learned how to change energy from fuels, such as coal, oil, and gas, into heat energy, which boils water. In power stations, machines change the energy of the steam from boiling water into electrical energy, which flows to our homes, factories, and stores. This electrical energy can then be transferred into light and heat or used to work other machines. As you can see from these pages, there are at least seven types of energy.

HEAT ENERGY
Everything is made of tiny particles called **molecules**. Heat energy, or thermal energy, causes the molecules of a substance to move around, or vibrate. When a substance is heated, its molecules begin to vibrate vigorously. When it cools down, its molecules vibrate more slowly. Heat is one way of moving energy from place to place. Heat energy flows from hot materials to cold ones and continues to flow until both materials are the same temperature.

LIGHT ENERGY
Light energy comes from any material that is hot enough to glow, such as the sun, electric lights, or burning objects. Light travels in a straight line as a stream of particles called photons and can pass through air, water, glass, and many other materials. We cannot see all forms of light. Some forms, such as infrared, ultraviolet, and X rays, are not visible. Light travels at very high speeds—about 186,000 miles (300,000 km) per second through space, which is a vacuum.

SOUND ENERGY
The sounds that we hear start when something makes the air vibrate, or move back and forth, quickly. The vibrations create sound waves in the air. Anything that vibrates, whether it is a bee's wings, a jet engine, or the human voice box, makes sounds.

MECHANICAL ENERGY
Mechanical energy deals with the way matter interacts with forces, such as **gravity**. Mechanical energy can be classified as kinetic energy, or energy of motion, and potential, or stored, energy.

MAKE A WINDMILL
To show the effects of an invisible force that turns into movement, make a windmill. You will need a paper plate, four paper cups, tape, a thumbtack, and a short stick.

1. Use the thumbtack to make a small hole in the center of the plate.

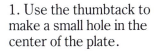

2. Tape the four paper cups evenly around the edge of the plate.

3. Attach the plate to the top of the stick with the thumbtack. See that the plate turns freely.

4. Blow into one of the cups. Watch how the wheel turns because of the air pushing the cups.

5. The energy comes from the moving air when you blow toward the cups.

ELECTRICAL ENERGY
Electrical energy is a convenient form of energy. It can be easily moved through wires, and it can readily be converted into other forms of energy.

CHEMICAL ENERGY
Chemicals are substances that make up materials. Chemical energy is stored in bonds that hold together the molecules that the materials are made of. This energy can be released when a chemical is made to react. For example, when coal or oil reacts with oxygen, the fuel burns and releases heat and light energy. The human body burns food slowly to produce the energy needed to move. Chemicals in a flashlight battery react to produce electrical energy.

NUCLEAR ENERGY
Nuclear energy is produced when changes occur in the nuclei, or centers, of atoms. Atomic nuclei of some substances decay, or break down, releasing very large amounts of energy, much of it in the form of heat. Substances whose nuclei decay naturally are said to be radioactive. Compared with other fuels, radioactive substances are concentrated sources of energy, which means that a lot of energy can be released from small amounts of radioactive material.

HOW DO WE KNOW

Where Energy Comes From?

All the energy on Earth originally comes from the sun. The sun produces tremendous amounts of energy, which streams out into space in all directions. Some of this energy finds its way to Earth.

Most of the sun's energy reaches the Earth in the form of visible light (sunlight), and invisible infrared and ultraviolet light. Light travels at about 186,000 miles (300,000 km) a second. Since the sun is 93 million miles (150 million km) from the Earth, light takes about 8 minutes to travel from the sun to the Earth. Scientists believe that nothing can travel faster than light.

The energy reaching the Earth heats its surface and atmosphere, making life possible on our planet. Without the energy from the sun, the Earth would be a frozen mass of ice and rock, where no living thing could survive. Sunlight is also used by plants to make their food, some of which is stored as energy in a chemical form. This is the source of the energy in our own food and the food of all other animals.

Scientists believe that the sun will shine for the next 5 billion years and then start to run out of hydrogen fuel. Slowly it will shrink and then die. At that point our solar system will also collapse.

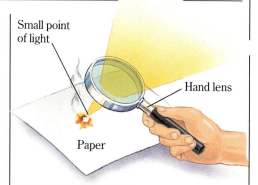

ENERGY FROM THE SUN
Take a magnifying glass outside on a sunny day. Hold the lens above a piece of paper. Move the lens until it forms a bright spot of light on the paper. Soon the paper will start to burn, as the sun's rays are concentrated on it.

THE SUN
The sun is a gigantic ball of gas, mostly hydrogen. It measures 865,000 miles (1,392,000 km) across, over 100 times the diameter of the Earth. The surface of the sun is called the photosphere, and the temperature there is about 11,000°F (6000°C). At the center, chemical **reactions** take place. In these reactions hydrogen atoms join together, or fuse, to form helium gas, producing vast amounts of energy. At the center of the sun, the temperature could be as high as 32,000,000°F (15,000,000°C.)

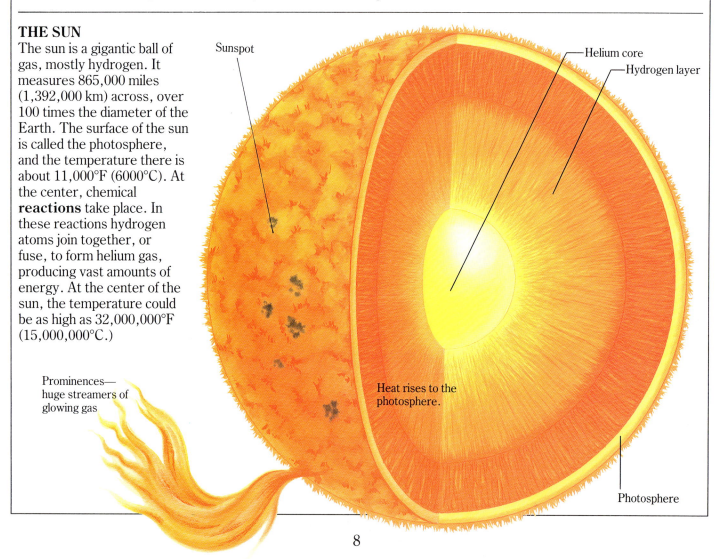

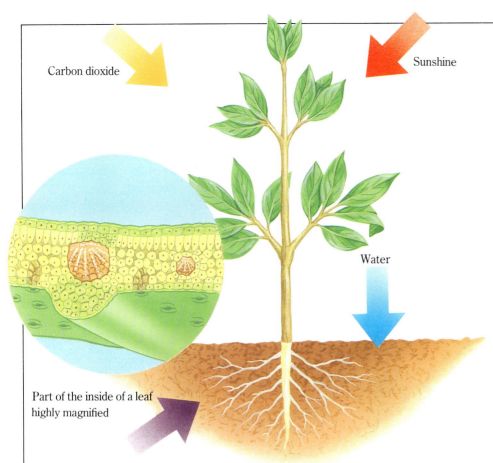

Carbon dioxide · Sunshine · Water · Part of the inside of a leaf highly magnified

HOW PLANTS MAKE THEIR FOOD

Plants make food by a process called photosynthesis, which uses energy from sunlight. Photosynthesis starts with the green pigment **chlorophyll**, which absorbs sunlight and converts it to chemical energy. A further reaction with carbon dioxide and water, taken from the air, produces sugars in the plant leaves. The plant uses some of the sugars as food. The rest is carried to other parts of the plant and stored as **starch**.

Photosynthesis not only produces food for plants and the animals that eat them, it also removes carbon dioxide gas from the air and releases oxygen. Animals need oxygen in order to carry out respiration, the process by which they breathe and burn food to provide energy.

GEOTHERMAL ENERGY

The interior of the Earth is extremely hot. In some volcanic parts of the world, there are very hot rocks near the surface. Heat from these rocks can be used at the surface to do work.

Heat that is tapped from below ground is called geothermal energy. It is used in parts of the United States, Iceland, New Zealand, Italy, and Japan, where hot water and steam rises to the surface as hot springs and **geysers**.

In other places, it is also possible to tap the heat from hot, dry rocks. Water is pumped down a geothermal well, where it is heated by the rocks and turns to steam. This steam rises up a second hole and can be used for heating or to generate electricity.

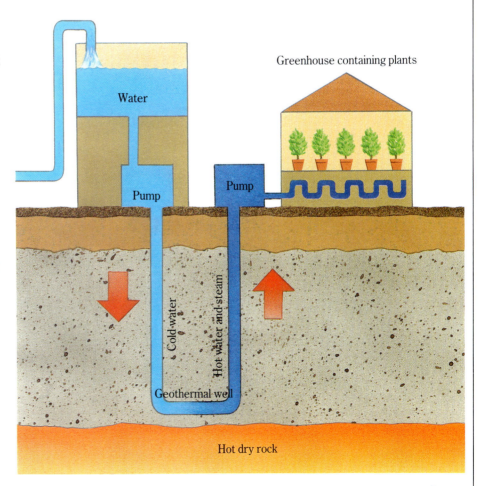

HOW DO WE KNOW

How to Use Energy?

We know how to convert energy and how to make energy work for us. Any form of work is energy being used. You see, hear, and feel the effects of energy doing work every day.

Electrical energy, for example, flows through wires and cables into appliances and devices, such as lamps and food mixers. It makes them work. The devices change electricity into other forms of energy. A lamp produces light and heat energy. You see movement, or mechanical energy, when food is stirred with a mixer.

As we have seen, energy exists in many forms, and it is often possible to change one form into another. We use these forms of energy to move our bodies, to keep warm, and to do work. However, although we may convert one kind of energy into another, we never make any new energy. And although we may use energy, it is never used up, or destroyed. Energy changes and may become spread around, but the total amount of energy always stays the same.

ENERGY CHANGES
Energy tends to travel along in a chainlike way as it changes from one form to another. One simple energy chain is:

Sun → wheat → bread → person → winding an alarm clock (movement energy) → stored energy in clock's spring → sound energy

As we have seen, nuclear reactions inside the sun release enormous amounts of energy, some of which travels to the Earth as light. Light energy is converted by wheat plants to make their own food. The grains or seeds from the wheat plant may be made into flour and then bread. When people eat the bread, they make their own store of chemical energy. If we use the energy from the bread to wind an alarm clock, the kinetic (movement) energy used in winding the clock is changed into potential, or stored energy, in the spring of the clock. As the spring unwinds, the energy released moves the hands of the clock. When the alarm goes off, the stored or potential energy turns into mechanical energy in the bell of the clock. The bell produces sound energy.

Weight lifting
Without the energy we get from food, our bodies would not be able to work. In the muscles of this weight lifter, the food chemicals that give energy are "burned" with oxygen that his body has taken from the air. When the heavy weights are lifted, some of the chemical energy of the food stored in the weight lifter's muscles is changed to movement, or kinetic energy. He feels very hot, because some of the food energy turns to heat energy.

Chemical energy
↓
Kinetic energy
↓
Heat energy

An electric light bulb
An electric light bulb turns electrical energy into light energy. Since the bulb gets very hot, we know that heat energy is also being produced. The electrical energy comes from a power station, where coal, oil, gas, or nuclear fuel is used to produce heat energy. This energy is then used to generate electricity.

Heat energy
↓
Electrical energy
↓
Light energy and heat energy

A radio receiver
At a radio station, a microphone changes sound energy into electrical signals. These are sent out as electromagnetic radio waves from the antenna of the transmitter. The antenna on the radio set picks up the radio waves, and these are turned back into sounds by the speaker in the radio receiver.

Sound energy
↓
Electrical energy
↓
Sound energy

SEE CHEMICAL ENERGY AT WORK
Pour a little vinegar into a jar. Then carefully spoon a little baking soda into it. Watch carefully.

The vinegar and the baking soda react together and make the gas carbon dioxide. This froths and bubbles as chemical energy is turned into the movement, or kinetic energy, of the bubbles. You should be able to feel the bottom of the jar become a little warmer as some of the chemical energy is turned into heat energy.

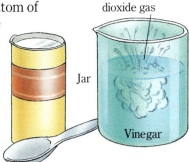

Bubbles of carbon dioxide gas
Jar
Bicarbonate of soda
Vinegar

Fireworks
Fireworks contain gunpowder, a fast-burning material that releases gases when it is burned. The rapid expansion of these gases produces an explosion. The gunpowder is really a store of chemical energy, and when the fireworks are lit, this chemical energy is changed to heat, light, and sound energy.

Chemical energy
↓
Heat, light, and sound energy

Electrical energy
↓
Light energy and sound energy

A television set
Television cameras take pictures and change them into electrical signals. There are different signals for red, blue, and green. The electrical signals are sent out to be picked up by an antenna on the television set or on the house roof. Inside the television set the electrical signals hit the screen and form the picture. Meanwhile the loudspeaker of the television set changes electrical signals into words and music.

Microphone
A microphone changes sound energy into electrical energy. Inside the microphone, sound waves strike a thin plate called a diaphragm. The diaphragm moves back and forth, or vibrates, at the same rate as the sound waves. The diaphragm is connected to a device that produces an electrical signal. This signal is carried from the microphone as an electric current.

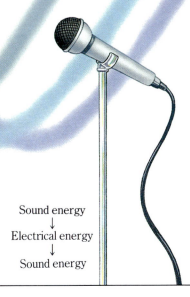

Sound energy
↓
Electrical energy
↓
Sound energy

Car engine
A car engine turns the chemical energy in fuel into movement, or kinetic energy. A great deal of sound energy and heat energy is produced, as well. The movement, or kinetic energy, is needed to make the car move. Most of the sound and heat is "wasted" energy.

Chemical energy
↓
Movement, sound, and heat energy

11

HOW DO WE KNOW

How to Store Energy?

Energy can be stored in many different materials and in a number of different ways. There is, for example, a lot of energy stored in food. Some animals store food in their bodies in the form of fat for use in the winter. Fuels, such as oil, coal, gas, and wood, also contain stored energy. In all these examples energy is stored as chemical energy.

There are other ways in which energy can be stored. It can, for example, be stored in a coiled spring or in stretched elastic. These materials have energy because they are trying to return to their original shapes.

Stored energy is called potential energy. If you climb to the top of a slide and sit there, you have stored the energy you used to get there. If you then let go, the stored or potential energy is changed back into kinetic or movement energy as you rush down the slide. Potential energy is really the energy an object (or person) has because of its position. A ball resting on the ground has no energy, but if the ball is held in the air, it has potential energy. Of course, this type of potential energy relies on the force of gravity to make it work.

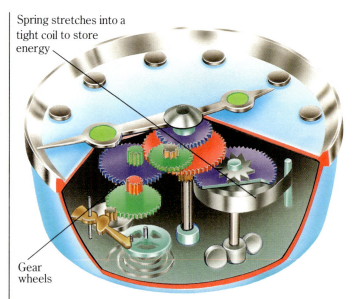

HOW A CLOCK SPRING STORES ENERGY

When you wind up a clock or watch, you are using chemical energy in your muscles to stretch the spring inside it into a tight coil. Later the energy stored in the coiled spring is slowly released as kinetic (movement) energy that turns the gear wheels and the hands on the face of the clock or watch.

Hydroelectric power

Rain falling on high ground finds it way into rivers and streams, which flow down to sea level. A built-up dam stops the water, and a large lake, or reservoir, soon collects behind it. The dam controls the flow of water. The water, by having its level raised, gains potential energy.

When electricity is needed, **valves** in the dam allow some of the water to fall down through large fans, or **turbines**. The potential energy of the water is changed to kinetic energy. The fast-flowing water turns the turbines, which are connected to **generators**. These turn and produce electricity.

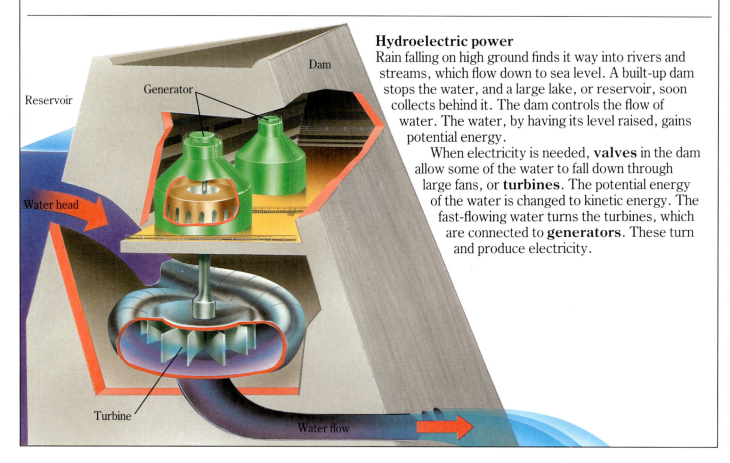

WORKING WITH A HEAVY WEIGHT

Tall buildings have to be built on firm foundations to stop them from sinking, toppling over, or cracking apart. The taller the building, the deeper its foundations need to be.

Most tall buildings are built on columns, called piles, sunk deep into the ground. A pile driver is the machine used to do this. It relies on the kinetic energy of a large weight dropped from a height. The weight is raised on the arm of the pile driver, giving it potential energy. The weight is then dropped onto the top of the pile, giving it kinetic energy. Repeated blows of this kind eventually drive the pile deep into the ground. When many piles have been sunk into the ground, the building can then be constructed on top.

Pile tower

Hydraulic arm

Weight

Pile

Pile is driven into the ground

MAKE A THREAD SPOOL WINDUP TOY

A windup toy shows how much energy is stored in a rubber band. You will need a thread spool, a rubber band, a paper clip, a stick, and a thin slice of candle wax with the wick removed.

Piece of candle

1. Thread the rubber band through the hole in the spool. Fasten one end to the paper clip.

Rubber band

2. Make a hole in the center of the piece of candle. Pass the rubber band through it. Then pull the stick through the rubber band and hold it in place with a paper clip.

Thread spool

3. Wind up the rubber band by turning the stick. Put the toy on the floor, and see how far it will go. Does your windup toy work equally well on both smooth and rough surfaces?

Stick

HOW DO WE KNOW

What Slows Things Down?

No matter how hard you roll a ball along the ground, it will stop rolling. Moving objects slow down and stop because, when energy changes from one form to another, some energy is always "lost." That is, it changes into forms of energy other than kinetic energy.

The main reason for this energy loss is friction. This is a force that tends to stop objects from sliding past each other. Friction often wastes kinetic energy by changing it into heat and sound energy.

Friction can also be very useful. For example, the friction between a car's tires and the road allows the tires to grip the road and to stop the car from skidding. Friction also makes nails stay in wood when they are hammered in. However, if two moving parts of a machine rub against each other, the friction can cause them to wear away. Oil or grease and ball bearings can be used as **lubricants** so that metal surfaces do not rub directly against each other.

Friction does not only occur when solid materials rub against each other. There is also friction between moving objects and air or water moving past them.

Raise slowly — Smooth wooden board

SEE HOW FRICTION WORKS
You will need a smooth wooden board, an ice cube, a rubber eraser, a small block of wood, a piece of clay or plasticine, a small box, and a toy car. Arrange the objects in a line at one end of the board. Carefully raise that end of the board a little bit at a time. The objects with less friction will move first, and those with the most friction will move last.

BRAKES
A bicycle's brakes work because of friction. When the brakes are applied, the brake pads and the rim of the bicycle wheel rub against each other to slow the bicycle down. The harder you squeeze the brake handles, the greater the friction, and the faster the wheel slows down.

A car's brakes are operated when the driver pushes the brake pedal down. Most modern cars have disc brakes, at least on the front wheels. In disc brakes, a pair of metal brake pads press against a metal disc attached to the wheel. The friction between the two stops the wheel.

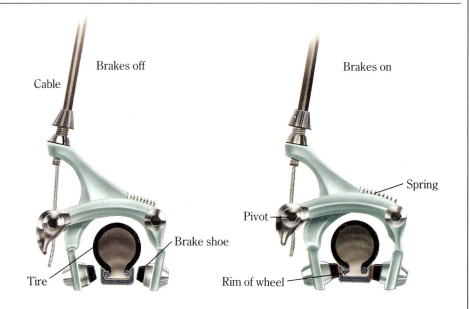

Old car brakes
In old-fashioned drum brakes, when the driver pressed the brake pedal, a pair of curved brake shoes pressed against the brake drums on each wheel, creating friction, which stopped the wheels.

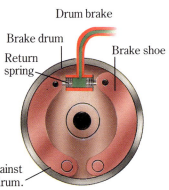

Bicycle brakes
When you squeeze on your bicycle brakes, it forces brake pads to rub against the rim of the wheel, slowing the bike down. The harder you squeeze, the quicker you stop.

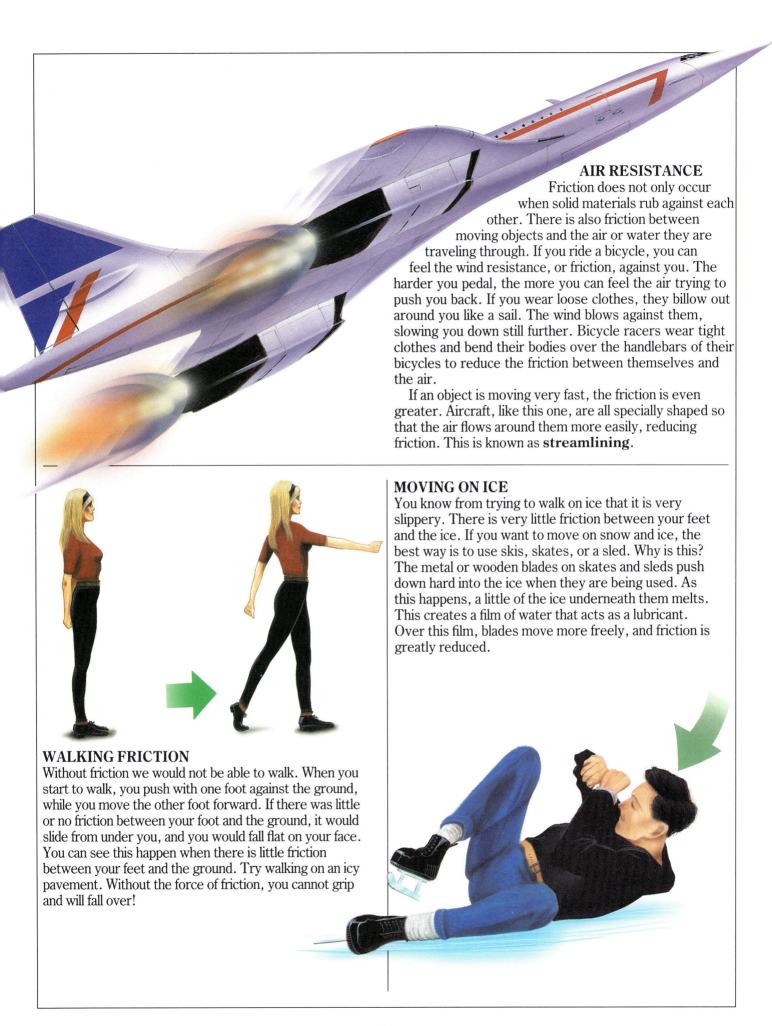

AIR RESISTANCE

Friction does not only occur when solid materials rub against each other. There is also friction between moving objects and the air or water they are traveling through. If you ride a bicycle, you can feel the wind resistance, or friction, against you. The harder you pedal, the more you can feel the air trying to push you back. If you wear loose clothes, they billow out around you like a sail. The wind blows against them, slowing you down still further. Bicycle racers wear tight clothes and bend their bodies over the handlebars of their bicycles to reduce the friction between themselves and the air.

If an object is moving very fast, the friction is even greater. Aircraft, like this one, are all specially shaped so that the air flows around them more easily, reducing friction. This is known as **streamlining**.

MOVING ON ICE

You know from trying to walk on ice that it is very slippery. There is very little friction between your feet and the ice. If you want to move on snow and ice, the best way is to use skis, skates, or a sled. Why is this? The metal or wooden blades on skates and sleds push down hard into the ice when they are being used. As this happens, a little of the ice underneath them melts. This creates a film of water that acts as a lubricant. Over this film, blades move more freely, and friction is greatly reduced.

WALKING FRICTION

Without friction we would not be able to walk. When you start to walk, you push with one foot against the ground, while you move the other foot forward. If there was little or no friction between your foot and the ground, it would slide from under you, and you would fall flat on your face. You can see this happen when there is little friction between your feet and the ground. Try walking on an icy pavement. Without the force of friction, you cannot grip and will fall over!

HOW DO WE KNOW

Where Energy Goes?

Sometimes it seems as if energy is lost or used up. But in fact energy is never destroyed. It simply changes from one form to another or is moved from one place to another.

Heat seems to disappear more readily than other forms of energy. It is a form of energy that occurs in the movements and vibrations of the molecules that make up all materials. When a substance is heated, its molecules vibrate faster. When the substance cools down, its molecules vibrate slower.

The most obvious sign of the loss or gain of heat energy is a change of state. For example, if water is heated to 212°F (100°C), it boils and turns into water vapor (a gas). If water is cooled below 32°F (0°C), it turns into solid ice. A less obvious sign of heating or cooling materials is that they can get bigger or smaller. Nearly all substances get bigger, or expand, when heated and become smaller, or contract, when cooled. This is because more or less energy is in their atoms or molecules.

Heat energy flows from hot materials to cold ones. It continues to flow until the materials are at the same temperature, the measurement of hot or cold.

HOW HEAT TRAVELS

Heat travels from hot materials to cold ones. It does this in three main ways. Conduction is the way heat energy travels in solids and liquids. Some materials, such as metals, allow heat to pass through them easily and are called conductors (they conduct heat well). Others, such as wood, rubber, and plastic, do not allow an easy flow and are called insulators (they are bad conductors). The second way heat travels is convection. If the sun warms an area of land, the land warms the air above it. The molecules of the warm air move more quickly, and the air becomes lighter. The warm air rises, and cooler, heavier air takes its place. This type of heat transfer, which takes place in both gases and liquids, is called convection. Radiation is the third way heat travels. The heat energy travels in waves, like those of light. In fact it travels at the same speed as light.

Radiation
Heat travels by radiation in a stream of waves. The hotter something becomes, the more heat it radiates. Radiation does not depend on the movement of atoms or molecules, so it can travel through a complete vacuum.

Conduction
Heat travels from the burner throughout the pot as the vibration of one molecule is passed on to the next.

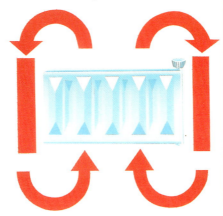

Convection
Although by its name a radiator sounds as though it transfers heat by radiation, in fact it is a convector. It makes the air in a room circulate by constantly heating it.

Conductors and insulators of heat
You will need a rubber hot water bottle and a selection of different materials, such as a plastic plate, a metal lid, a piece of wood, and a piece of cardboard. Ask an adult to fill the hot water bottle with hot water for you.

Lay the plastic plate on the hot water bottle. Carefully touch the plate with your hand. Notice that the plate does not warm up very quickly. Plastic is a heat insulator. Now try the same thing with the metal lid. Be careful! The lid quickly becomes hot. The metal is a good conductor of heat.

Try the others. Which are conductors, and which are insulators?

16

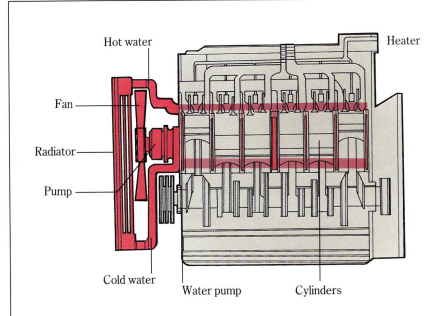

HOW A CAR ENGINE IS COOLED

Only about 15 percent of the energy stored in fuel is converted into mechanical energy to make the car move. The rest of the energy is changed into sound and heat. If the engine became too hot, the moving parts would expand and seize up. To keep this from happening, most cars have engines cooled by water. A pump drives the water around channels inside the engine. The hot water then passes to the car radiator and is cooled by the air blowing through it.

DISAPPEARING ENERGY

Many buildings, especially old ones, lose a great deal of heat to the outside by conduction, convection, and radiation. The picture shows the various ways in which a house can lose heat if it is not properly insulated with materials that prevent heat loss. There are several ways you can prevent heat loss from your home. The first is to make sure your roof is fully lined with a material called fiberglass. It is a wonderful insulator. Double-glazing helps stop heat from escaping through windows, and lining doors fills in the gaps where heat escapes.

Similarly, a light bulb "wastes" 90 percent of the electrical energy it uses as heat. Only 10 percent of the electrical energy is turned into light energy. Fluorescent tubes are more effective with only 60 percent of the electrical energy being wasted as heat.

HOW DO WE KNOW

Sound Is Energy?

When you switch on a radio, its loudspeaker sends ripples of sound through the air in all directions. These ripples move air molecules and are called sound waves. The moving air molecules are not the sound, but without them there is silence.

Sounds can travel only if there are molecules around to move. In space there are no air molecules, so astronauts have to talk to each other by radio. Radio waves, like light waves, can travel through a perfectly empty space.

Sound travels faster through solids and liquids than through air. Native Americans knew this, and they used to place their ears against the ground to listen for the sound of approaching horses. They knew that the sound of hoofbeats would reach them more quickly through the solid ground than it would through air. At 68°F (20°C), sound travels through air at about 1,900 miles per hour (3,058 kph) and through water at about 8,400 miles per hour (13,518 kph).

HOW WE HEAR SOUNDS

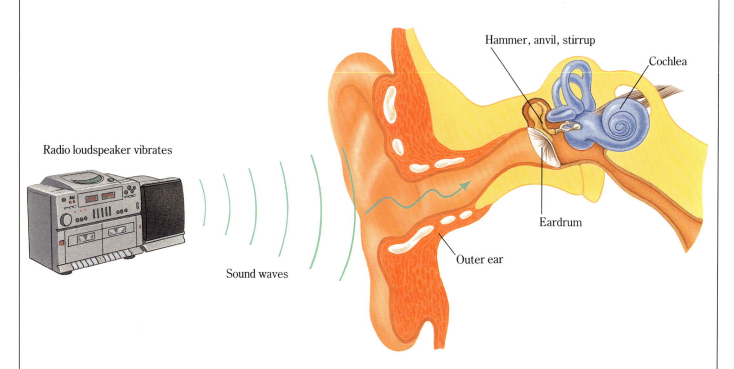

We use our ears to hear sound. The outer ear, the part we can see, collects sound waves and passes them down a canal to the eardrum. The eardrum vibrates when the sound waves hit it, and the vibrations are passed on to three tiny bones: the hammer, the anvil, and the stirrup. These three bones carry the vibrations to the inner ear. From here the vibrations pass into a coiled, liquid-filled tube called the cochlea, where highly sensitive cells pick up the vibrations, and nerves carry the electrical signals to the brain, where the sounds are identified.

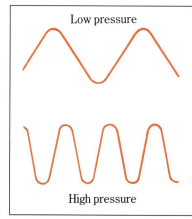

SOUND WAVES
When an object vibrates, air molecules touching it are forced to move closer together. As they travel away from the object, they spread apart in all directions. This creates areas of high and low pressure in the air, which make up sound waves.

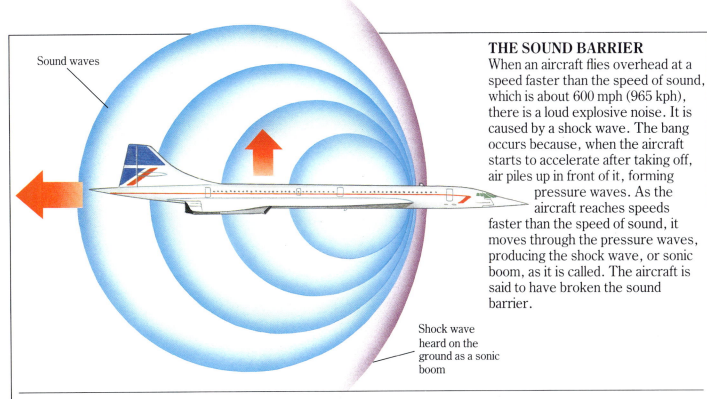

Sound waves

Shock wave heard on the ground as a sonic boom

THE SOUND BARRIER
When an aircraft flies overhead at a speed faster than the speed of sound, which is about 600 mph (965 kph), there is a loud explosive noise. It is caused by a shock wave. The bang occurs because, when the aircraft starts to accelerate after taking off, air piles up in front of it, forming pressure waves. As the aircraft reaches speeds faster than the speed of sound, it moves through the pressure waves, producing the shock wave, or sonic boom, as it is called. The aircraft is said to have broken the sound barrier.

THE PATTERN MADE BY SOUND
Scientists use an oscilloscope to record sounds, especially those we can't hear. When a microphone is connected to the oscilloscope, the instrument changes sound vibrations into electrical signals. These in turn are changed into wavelike patterns on the screen.

The pattern of waves on the screen tells the scientist about the sounds making the pattern. The taller the waves, the louder the sounds. The more waves there are on the screen, the more sound waves passing the microphone in a second. This pattern is produced by high-pitched sounds. Low-pitched sounds produce only a few waves.

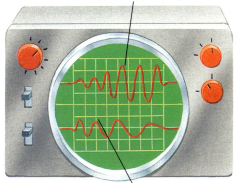

Tall waves show loud sounds.

Oscilloscope

Short waves show soft sounds.

USING ECHOES
Echoes are produced when sound waves bounce off a solid surface. The farther the source of the sound is from the solid surface, the longer the echo takes to come back. A **sonar machine** is used on boats to find the depth of anything beneath them. Sonar can measure the depth of the seabed as well as locate schools of fish, submarines, and wrecked ships.

A device under the ship sends pulses of sound down through the water. Any object in the water sends back an echo. A receiver measures the time delay of the signals and their strength. On a screen it shows how deep and how solid the objects causing the echoes are.

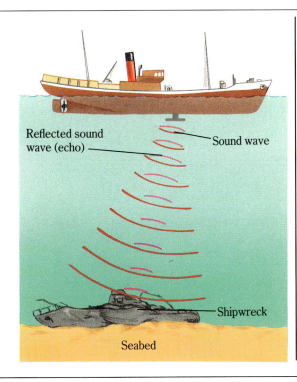

Reflected sound wave (echo)
Sound wave
Shipwreck
Seabed

Book
Ruler
Vibrations

Making vibrations with a flexible ruler
Hold the book over one end of the ruler on the edge of a table. Flick the other end of the ruler. Listen to the sound the ruler makes. Change the length of the ruler. Notice that when only a short piece of the ruler is vibrating, a high sound is made. A long piece of ruler makes a low sound when flicked.

HOW DO WE KNOW

Light Is Energy?

Light comes from the sun or other objects that are very hot or burning, such as an electric light bulb. Light can travel through **transparent** materials, such as air, water, or glass, but it reflects off solid objects. We see these objects when the reflected light enters our eyes. Without light we wouldn't be able to see anything.

Light travels in straight lines. Scientists believe that it travels in waves. These waves can travel through empty space. Unlike sound waves, light waves do not need the movement of any other material, such as air or water, to carry them.

Light waves belong to a family of waves called the electromagnetic spectrum. In addition to the light we can see (visible light), the electromagnetic spectrum includes invisible ultraviolet rays, infrared rays, X rays, microwaves, and television and radio waves. They all travel at the same very high speed of over 186,000 miles (300,000 km) per second. Nothing in the universe travels as fast as light.

Sources of light
Here are some examples of everyday light sources. Most objects do not produce their own light. Instead they reflect light produced by other objects. The moon and the planets appear to give off light, but this is only because they reflect the sun's light. Good reflectors include mirrors and other shiny objects. But nearly everything we see reflects some light.

As we have seen, most light comes from hot objects. There are exceptions, however. Glowworms and fireflies produce a greenish, heatless light, which is produced by the effect of chemicals in the animals' bodies. It is a much more efficient way of making light than any we use, since there is no "waste" of energy in the form of heat.

LASERS
A laser is a device that produces an intense beam of colored light. The beam is different from that which an ordinary lamp can produce, in that it is just one, pure color, and the light waves all move at the same wavelength and frequency.

Lasers have many uses. These include reading the bar codes at some supermarket check-out counters, enabling compact disc players to work, sending some kinds of telephone signals, and guiding military missiles. In hospitals, lasers are used to burn away birthmarks and some cancer cells, while in industry they are used to cut metal and glass.

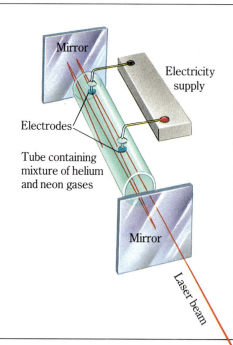

RAINBOWS

Ordinary white light from the sun is really a mixture of different colors, and each color has a different wavelength. When a ray of sunlight passes through a raindrop, the raindrop bends the light. Some colors bend more than others, and they spread out, forming a rainbow. These colors form the visible spectrum.

20

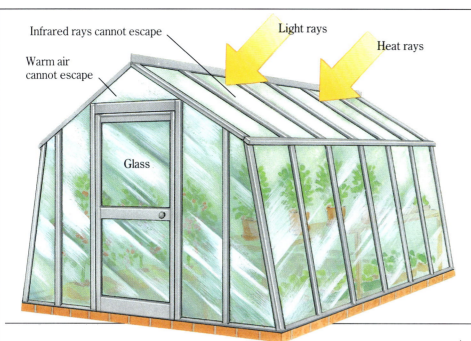

GREENHOUSES
Glass allows light rays to pass through easily but prevents heat (in the form of infrared rays) from passing. Thus the sun's light can pass readily into a greenhouse. Inside the greenhouse the light warms the soil, plants, and air. But the infrared rays given off by the heated soil and plants cannot pass through glass, and as most of the warmed air cannot escape either, the greenhouse acts as a heat trap.

HOW WE SEE
The eye is a hollow ball filled with fluid. At the front there is a round opening, called the pupil, that lets in light. The pupil is covered by a transparent layer known as the cornea. Behind the pupil is the lens. The eye focuses light by changing the shape of the lens. When the eye focuses on an object far away, the lens is flattened. When focusing on a near object, the lens is more rounded.

At the back of the eye, the light falls on the light-sensitive cells that form the retina. The image formed on the retina is upside down, but the retina sends messages to the brain, which then turns the picture right side up.

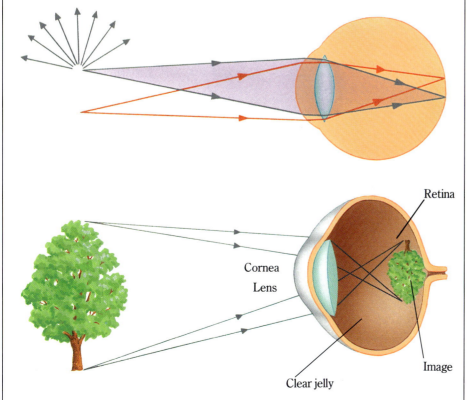

SHADOWS
Some materials, such as air, glass, and pure water, allow light to pass straight through them and are called transparent. Light cannot pass through objects such as wood, metal, or the human body. If you stand outside on a sunny day, the sun's rays cannot bend to go around your body, since the light travels in a straight line. A shadow in the shape of your body is made on the ground where the light does not reach.

21

HOW DO WE KNOW

Food Stores Energy?

Your body uses energy for every action. But your body cannot make this energy from nothing. It has to come from somewhere.

After you have walked or bicycled a long way or played an energetic sport, you may feel hungry. Hunger is your body's way of telling you that you need food to replace all the chemical energy you have used.

The food you eat comes from either plants or from other animals that have fed on plants. Plants are the only living things able to use sunlight energy and to produce and store chemical energy.

Our food contains five main groups of chemicals: carbohydrates, fats, proteins, vitamins, and minerals. Carbohydrates are foods that contain starch or sugar, such as bread, cakes, and candy. Fats include milk, butter, and cheese. Oils are liquid fats. Fats are the most concentrated form of energy. If you eat more food than your body really needs for energy, it stores the extra as fat.

FOOD CHAINS

As animals (including humans) cannot make their own food, they get energy by eating plants or by eating animals that have eaten plants. In doing so, energy passes from the plant to the animal that eats it. This energy came originally from the sun. Scientists call this energy flow through living things a food chain.

A food chain shows the sequence of who eats what. The chain always starts with plants. Animals are grouped by what they eat. Herbivores (plant-eaters) are near the bottom of food chains. They can be very small or very large animals, varying from tiny insects to cows, horses, and elephants. Some carnivores (meat-eaters) feed on herbivores, like ladybugs eating aphids, or lions feeding on antelope. Some carnivores eat other carnivores. They tend to be larger, fiercer, and rarer than the carnivores that eat herbivores.

MEASURING ENERGY FROM FOOD
Scientists have worked out a way of measuring the amount of energy given off by various foods. They found during their experiments that foods like cakes, potatoes, and candy (which all contain high amounts of carbohydrates) give off more energy than fresh fruit and vegetables. However, if you eat too many carbohydrates you get fat. The amount of calories we need in a normal diet, however, varies according to our age or way of life. The food shown here amounts to about 2,300 calories, which is just right for a growing 10–15 year old.

Breakfast is an important meal because it starts you up in the morning.

Always mix what you eat. Have carbohydrates, proteins, and fats.

HOW OUR FOOD PRODUCES ENERGY

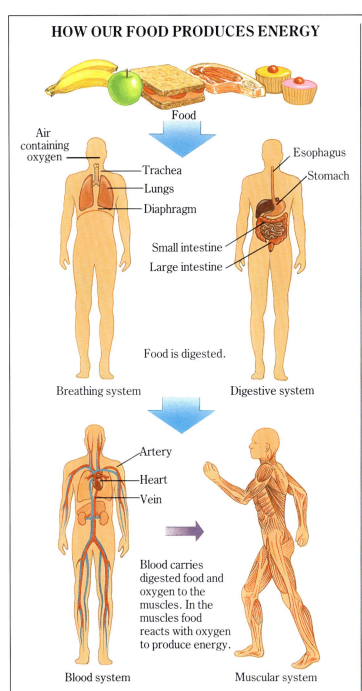

FOOD WEBS

The food chain is a simple way of showing how energy is passed from plants to animals. Most plants, however, are eaten by many kinds of animals, and most animals eat several kinds of food. Food chains usually have many branches, which scientists call a food web.

Food webs rarely have more than four or five layers. The reason is that with each layer, the amount of energy transferred gets smaller. This is because some of it has already been used up by the animal or plant as it is living and growing.

Food has to go through a number of complicated processes before you can use the stored chemical energy it contains. After you swallow food, it begins a long journey through the digestive system, which stretches about 23 feet (7 m) from the mouth to the stomach and on to the anus. In the digestive system, the useful food is broken down by chemicals so that it can pass through the walls of the digestive system into the blood. The food that is not useful to the body is passed out of the anus.

Before it can give off energy, the food has to be combined with oxygen, which is taken from the air by your lungs when you breathe and carried around the body by the blood. In your muscles, the digested food and oxygen react chemically, producing the energy you need for your daily activities.

MAKE YOUR OWN FOOD CHAIN

This is a food chain you can study in the summer. Put a plant shoot with **aphids** on it in a small bottle of water. Put cotton around the top of the bottle to keep the insects from falling in. Put the bottle into a large jar. Add a ladybug.

Cover the jar with a lid that allows air to pass through. The aphids suck the juices of the plant. And the ladybug eats the aphids.

23

HOW DO WE KNOW

Prehistoric Trees Provide Today's Energy?

A fuel is something that releases heat energy as it burns with oxygen gas from the air. The first fuel, and the one that is still used a great deal all over the world, is wood. Wood comes from trees, which, like all plants, grow by using sunlight to make chemical energy.

The most widely used fuels today are fossil fuels: coal, oil, and gas. Fossil fuels were formed from living things that died millions of years ago. Coal was formed from dead plants that lived in prehistoric **swamps**. Animals, as well as plants, died and settled on the seabed and became buried millions of years ago. Pressure and the Earth's heat changed the decaying materials into oil and gas. Whether we cook our food on a fire of burning wood or charcoal (which is made from wood), or if we use a stove heated by coal, oil, or gas, we are using energy which came from sunlight millions of years ago.

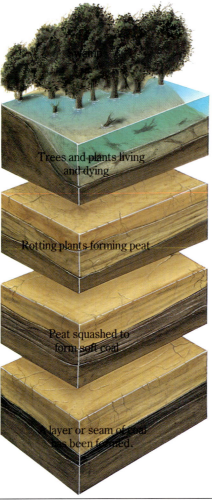

Trees and plants living and dying

Rotting plants forming peat

Peat squashed to form soft coal

Layer or seam of coal has been formed.

HOW COAL WAS FORMED
About 350 million years ago, parts of the Earth were covered with swamps. Dead plants rotted and slowly changed into peat, a rich heavy soil. Gradually the peat became buried under sand and mud, which were pressed down tightly, forming rock. The pressure of the rock above and the Earth's heat slowly changed the peat into layers of the black rock we call coal.

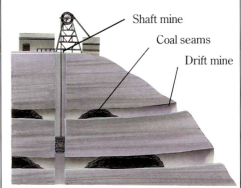

Shaft mine
Coal seams
Drift mine

How coal is mined
Coal near the surface is dug out with bulldozers. Coal seams mined underground are connected to the surface by sloping tunnels, or shaft mines are dug straight down to the coal seam.

FOSSIL PLANTS
A fossil is any remains or trace of a plant or animal that lived millions of years ago, such as a leaf, shell, bone, or footprint. Some fossils are preserved in rock by gradually being changed into rock themselves.

The plant fossils shown in the picture are parts of the trees and giant ferns that grew in vast damp forests. When the forests eventually dried out, most of the plants also died out.

HOW A COAL-FIRED POWER STATION WORKS

The electricity that we use comes from a power station. Inside the power station, huge boilers raise steam to a high pressure. The boiler is heated by burning coal.

The steam goes to the turbines. These are huge fans whose blades are turned by the pressure of the steam. As each turbine turns, it spins a generator, which consists of a **shaft** on which a large magnet turns inside coils of wire. As the magnet spins, it produces a powerful electric current in the coils of wire. The electric current flows out to power lines that take the electricity to homes and factories.

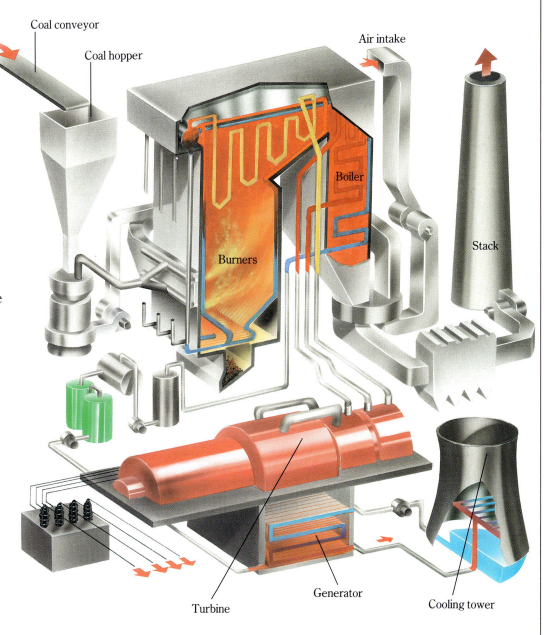

HOW OIL WAS FORMED

Oil was formed from the remains of tiny plants and animals that lived in the ocean millions of years ago. Today oil and gas can be found on land as well as under the sea. To reach the oil and gas, holes are drilled down to the **deposits** and lined with pipes. The oil and gas flow up these pipes, either naturally or they are pumped up.

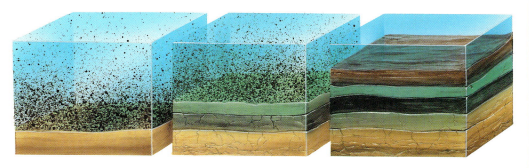

Dead sea creatures
When they died, the plants and animals sank to the sea-bed and were slowly covered with layers of sand and mud.

Layers of rock
The sand and mud slowly changed into rocks as their weight became heavier. This pressed down hard on the remains of the plants and animals.

Oil and gas form
Buried deep underground, these remains gradually became very hot and eventually turned into oil and gas.

25

HOW DO WE KNOW

Wind and Rain Can Make Electricity?

Tremendous amounts of energy reach Earth from the sun every day. This energy heats regions near the equator more effectively than it does regions near the poles. Thus, equatorial regions are much warmer. As the air over these regions is heated, it expands and becomes less dense. Cooler air moves in and forces the warm air to rise in **convection currents**. These air movements cause systems of winds to form and influence weather patterns worldwide.

The total amount of water present on Earth doesn't change. The same water is continually circulating between the Earth's surface and the atmosphere. This so-called water cycle is driven by the sun's energy. Moving air, or wind, and moving water have energy. Some of this energy can be captured by various devices and converted to other forms of energy that are useful to our life-styles. For example, windmills convert the wind energy into mechanical energy that can be used to pump water or generate electricity.

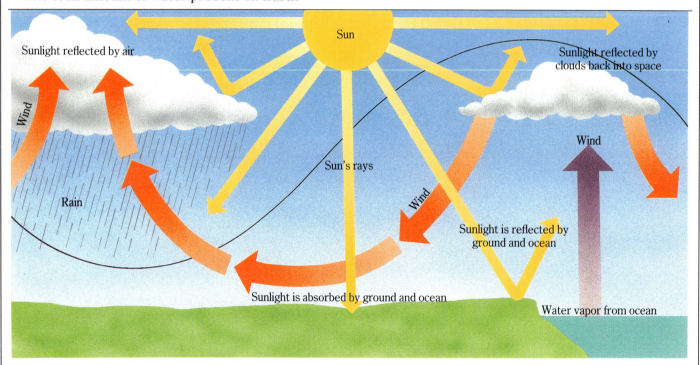

THE WATER CYCLE

During the water cycle, heat from the sun evaporates water from the oceans, lakes, and rivers, and from all other damp surfaces, forming water vapor in the air. As moist air rises, it cools. The water vapor condenses, or becomes liquid again, forming clouds. As the clouds cool still further, the water droplets in them get bigger. Eventually they fall as rain, hail, sleet, or snow. This precipitation collects in streams and rivers, which flow toward the ocean, enabling the whole water cycle to begin all over again. There is a great deal of kinetic energy in the moving waters of rivers, which can be used in hydroelectric power stations. These power stations use moving water to turn turbines, which generate electricity.

There are also vast amounts of kinetic energy in the rising and falling of the tides. Tides are caused by several forces, the most important of which is the moon's gravity. This pull causes the ocean's water to pile up on the side of the Earth that faces the moon. The highest and lowest tides are called spring tides.

Waves are caused by the wind. They do not move the seawater from place to place like currents and tides. Although a wave is just a big ripple of water made by the wind, it does have a great deal of kinetic energy.

WIND POWER

For hundreds of years wind power was used by windmills for grinding corn or pumping water. Today large windmills, or wind turbines, with blades like huge aircraft propellers, are built to produce electricity. The blades turn a shaft that is connected to an electrical generator on top of the windmill. The larger windmills have an automatic control system that turns the head of the windmill toward the wind.

Wind power relies on the strength of the wind, which varies from day to day. However, it is a source of energy that does not pollute the atmosphere as burning coal, oil, and gas do.

A TIDAL POWER STATION

The energy in the tides can be harnessed by building a barrage, a kind of dam, across the mouth or estuary of a river. As the tides rise and fall, water flows in and out of the river mouth and is used to turn turbines in the barrage.

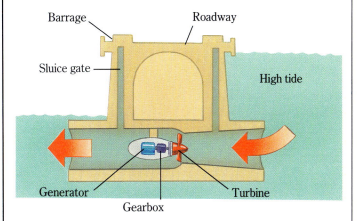

ELECTRICITY FROM THE WAVES

There are several different kinds of machines for catching the energy of waves. One kind of wave generator, shown here, consists of large floating rafts. Between one raft and the next, there is a cylinder containing a **piston** surrounded by liquid. This is called the hydraulic ram. The waves move the rafts, and the rafts move the rams. These cause a turbine and generator to turn, and so produce electricity.

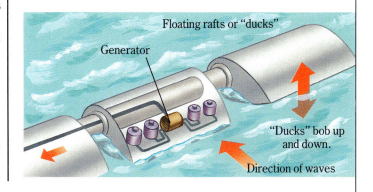

MAKE A MODEL TURBINE

To make a model turbine you will need the metal foil top from a yogurt container, a knitting needle, and scissors. Make a small hole in the center of the metal foil top. Cut eight slits at equal distances apart around the edge. Bend the eight pieces to make paddles. Push the knitting needle through the hole. Allow the water from a trickling water tap to fall on the paddles.

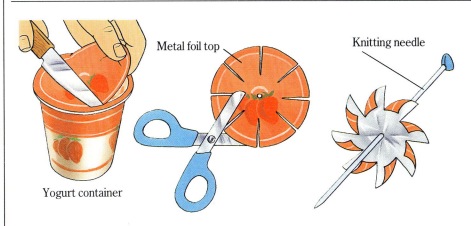

HOW DO WE KNOW

Electricity Gives Us Light and Heat?

Like heat, electricity flows more easily through some materials than others. Electricity flows most easily through metals, such as copper, iron, and tin. These materials are called conductors of electricity. Some materials, such as plastic and rubber, slow down the flow of electricity. They are called insulators of electricity. Copper is the metal most often used in electrical wires, since it is a good conductor. Wires, as well as electrical plugs and sockets, are covered with plastic, which insulates them and makes them safe to touch.

Good conductors of electricity allow **electrons** to flow easily. As the electrons flow, they collide with the **atoms** a wire is made of, and this slows them down. This slowing effect is called the wire's resistance. The longer or thinner the wire is, the more resistance it has. A thick wire has a lower resistance than a thin wire. In a thick wire there is a larger area for the electrons to pass along. It is like a highway, which can carry more traffic than a narrow country road. There is one big difference, though. In a thin wire, if a large number of electrons (a big electric current) hits the atoms in the wire, it makes them vibrate more, and the wire may get very hot.

AN ELECTRIC LIGHT BULB
When you switch on a light, electricity moves through the switch to the light bulb. In the bulb is a very thin, coiled wire called the filament. When electricity passes through the filament, it makes it so hot that it glows. A bright bulb uses more electricity than a less bright bulb. The brightness of a light bulb is measured in watts. A medium-sized room needs a bulb rated at about 100 watts.

The filament
The filament is made of a metal called tungsten. It has a very high melting point, which means that it does not melt when it becomes very hot. The filament glows because it has a high resistance to electricity. Electrons passing along the filament keep bumping into the tungsten atoms. The atoms vibrate rapidly and give off heat and light.

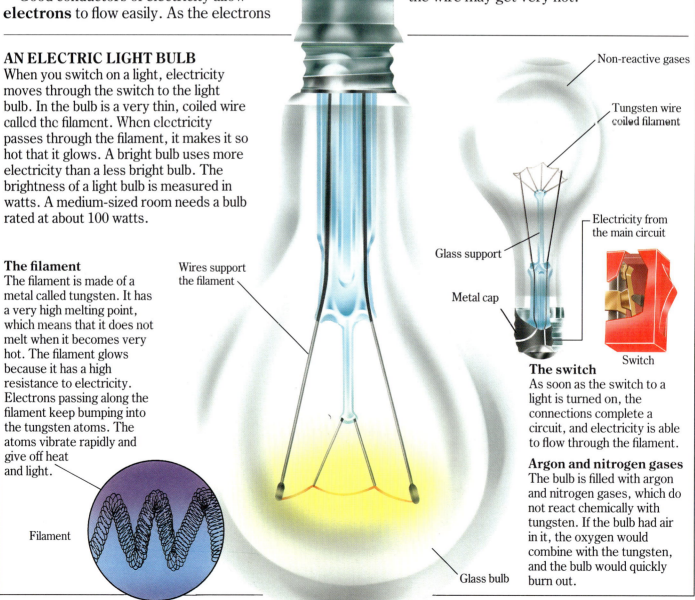

Filament

Wires support the filament

Non-reactive gases

Tungsten wire coiled filament

Glass support

Metal cap

Electricity from the main circuit

Switch

The switch
As soon as the switch to a light is turned on, the connections complete a circuit, and electricity is able to flow through the filament.

Argon and nitrogen gases
The bulb is filled with argon and nitrogen gases, which do not react chemically with tungsten. If the bulb had air in it, the oxygen would combine with the tungsten, and the bulb would quickly burn out.

Glass bulb

FLUORESCENT LIGHT BULBS

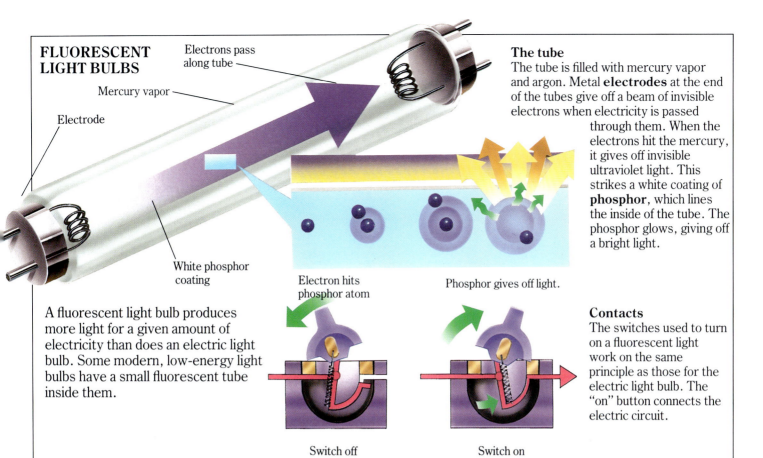

A fluorescent light bulb produces more light for a given amount of electricity than does an electric light bulb. Some modern, low-energy light bulbs have a small fluorescent tube inside them.

The tube
The tube is filled with mercury vapor and argon. Metal **electrodes** at the end of the tubes give off a beam of invisible electrons when electricity is passed through them. When the electrons hit the mercury, it gives off invisible ultraviolet light. This strikes a white coating of **phosphor**, which lines the inside of the tube. The phosphor glows, giving off a bright light.

Contacts
The switches used to turn on a fluorescent light work on the same principle as those for the electric light bulb. The "on" button connects the electric circuit.

ELECTRIC HEATERS

An electric heater is really just a long piece of thin wire made from a mixture of metals, an alloy, called nichrome. The wire, which has a high resistance, is wound around rods made of an insulator, such as porcelain. Porcelain is a substance that can be heated to a very high temperature without melting or bending. When electricity flows through the wire, the wire gets hot. It also heats up the porcelain. The wire used in the cord leading to the electric fire is made of much thicker copper, which has a lower resistance to electricity and does not get hot.

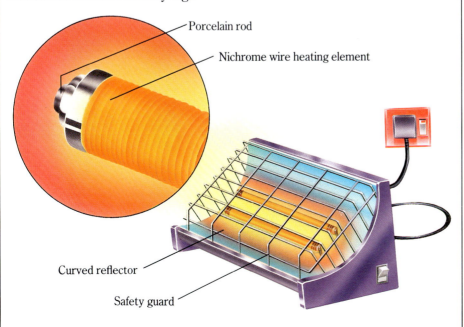

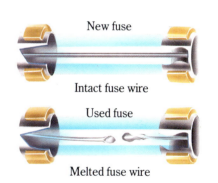

HOW FUSES WORK

The heating effect of an electric current can be very useful. But it could also be very dangerous. If there is a short in an electrical circuit, too much electricity could flow through a wire, causing damage or even starting a fire. To prevent these things from happening, fuses are used.

A fuse is a thin wire in a circuit that has a low melting point. If the correct amount of electricity passes along the circuit, the fuse stays intact. If too much electricity flows, the fuse heats up quickly and melts, cutting off the supply of electricity.

HOW DO WE KNOW

How Energy Gets into a Battery?

Electricity in transmission lines is very powerful, always needs wires and connectors, and can be dangerous if handled incorrectly. For items like portable radios and flashlights, which need relatively small amounts of electricity, a battery is much more convenient than the electricity supply.

The word *battery* is often misused. Technically the individual small cylinders that supply electricity to a flashlight are known as cells. A true battery is a number of electric cells joined together. The first electric cell was made in 1794 by Alessandro Volta, an Italian physicist. He discovered that if he connected two strips of different metals in salty water, an electric current passed along the wire. Even today's cells generate electric current because of chemical changes.

There are two main kinds of electric cells. The primary cell gives an electric current until the chemicals inside it are used up. It cannot be recharged. The secondary, or storage, cell can be recharged with electricity when it has run down.

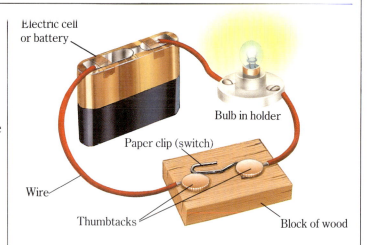

A SIMPLE ELECTRICAL CIRCUIT
An electrical circuit is a loop of wires through which an electric current can flow without interruption. All lights and other electrical appliances use a circuit. This is a simple electrical circuit. Press the switch down, and the circuit is completed. You can tell because the light goes on. NEVER PLAY WITH HOUSEHOLD ELECTRICITY. IT COULD KILL YOU.

INSIDE A CAR BATTERY
A car battery does not normally run out of electricity, because it can be recharged by a generator, which is turned by the engine when it is running. The car battery is designed to produce the strong electrical current needed to turn the car's starter motor. It does this by using a number of cells linked together.

Within each cell there are plates arranged in pairs. One plate of each pair is made of the metal lead, the other of the chemical lead oxide. These pairs of plates are suspended in dilute acid. Separator plates keep them apart, and dividers group the plates into cells within the battery.

To produce an electric current, the acid attacks the plates. It changes the chemical makeup of the plates. As it does so, tiny particles, called electrons, flow between the plates, causing an electric current. This kind of battery is sometimes called a storage battery.

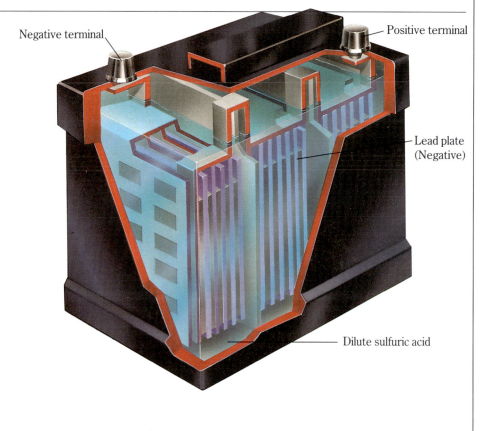

HOW A FLASHLIGHT WORKS

A flashlight is a useful light to carry around with you at night. The flashlight in the picture has a plastic case and, like all flashlights, instead of wires it has strips of metal along the sides of the case and a wire spring at its base. The wire spring pushes the two cells together and up against the base of the bulb. As with all electrical circuits, all connections in the flashlight must be tight, clean, and free from rust and grease. Like all switches, the switch of the flashlight makes a gap in the circuit when the flashlight is off and completes the circuit when the flashlight is on.

Bulb

Plastic case

Cells

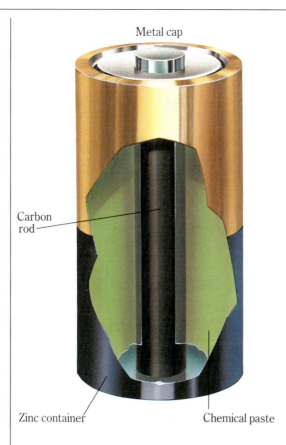

Metal cap

Carbon rod

Zinc container

Chemical paste

INSIDE A DRY CELL

The car battery contains sulfuric acid, which is easily spilled and can corrode metals and cloth or burn the skin. The dry cell used in flashlights contains a damp chemical paste called electrolyte. The cell's container is made of the metal zinc, and there is a carbon rod down the center. The carbon rod has a metal cap to help make a better electrical connection. When the dry cell is placed inside a flashlight and switched on, a chemical reaction that generates an electric current occurs in the paste.

A SIMPLE ELECTRIC MOTOR

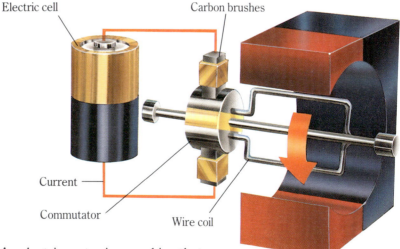

Electric cell

Carbon brushes

Current

Commutator

Wire coil

An electric motor is a machine that converts electrical energy into mechanical energy. An electric motor consists of a coil of wire held in the magnetic field of a permanent magnet. When an electric current is sent through the coil, the coil also becomes a magnet. The current is sent through in such a way that, to start with, the north pole of the magnet lines up with the north pole of the coil. Since like poles repel each other, and the magnet is stationary, the coil turns. It tries to line itself up with opposite poles together.

Just before the coil lines up with the north pole of the magnet facing the south pole of the coil, the flow of electricity is sent the other way by the commutator. So the two poles repel each other again, and the coil keeps turning in the same direction. The current keeps changing direction, so the coil keeps turning.

HOW DO WE KNOW

How to Imitate the Sun?

The sun generates energy through constant chemical reactions. To understand these, we need to get down to basics. Every substance in the universe, living or nonliving, is made up of tiny particles called atoms. An atom is so small that more than 4 billion would fit across the dot on top of the letter *i*. At the center of every atom is a nucleus. It is made up of very small particles, called protons and neutrons, packed tightly together. Very tiny particles, called electrons, move at high speed around the nucleus.

Some substances, such as iron or oxygen, are made up of just one kind of atom. Other substances, known as molecules, contain atoms joined together in groups. A water molecule, for example, contains two hydrogen atoms and one oxygen atom.

Nuclear energy, which is the energy found in the sun, is produced by the tiny particles in the nuclei of atoms. There are two different ways to obtain nuclear energy: nuclear fission and nuclear fusion.

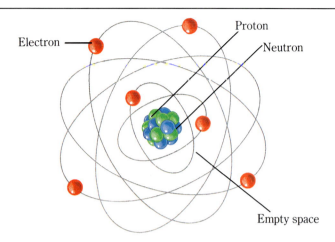

THE STRUCTURE OF THE ATOM
The nucleus in the center of an atom consists of protons and neutrons. These are held packed tightly together. Electrons whizz around the nucleus at very high speed and carry an electrical charge. Protons also carry a charge. However, it is a different kind of charge. While electrons carry a negative charge, protons carry a positive charge. Neutrons have no electric charge.

NUCLEAR REACTIONS IN THE SUN
The sun is a ball of hot gas, mainly hydrogen, with a lot of helium and smaller amounts of other gases. The energy that the sun releases as light and heat comes from processes of nuclear fusion, which take place near its center. In this process, nuclei of hydrogen atoms combine to form nuclei of helium atoms, and vast amounts of energy are given off in the process.

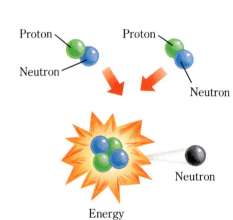

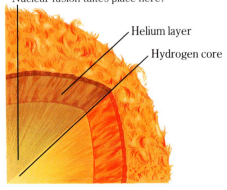

Nuclear fission
The energy in the element uranium cannot be released by burning. Instead, uranium nuclei are split into nuclei of smaller atoms to obtain energy. This process, called nuclear fission, can occur naturally in rock in the ground, but in a nuclear power station, a machine called a reactor speeds up and controls the process.

Nuclear fusion
Nuclear fusion is very difficult and expensive to achieve in the laboratory. Hydrogen atoms must be squeezed in a powerful magnetic field and maintained at a temperature higher than that at the sun's center for fusion to occur. When nuclear fusion does occur, though, it produces vast amounts of energy and only small amounts of radioactive waste. However, fusion is not widely used as yet, because it is so difficult to achieve.

INSIDE A NUCLEAR REACTOR

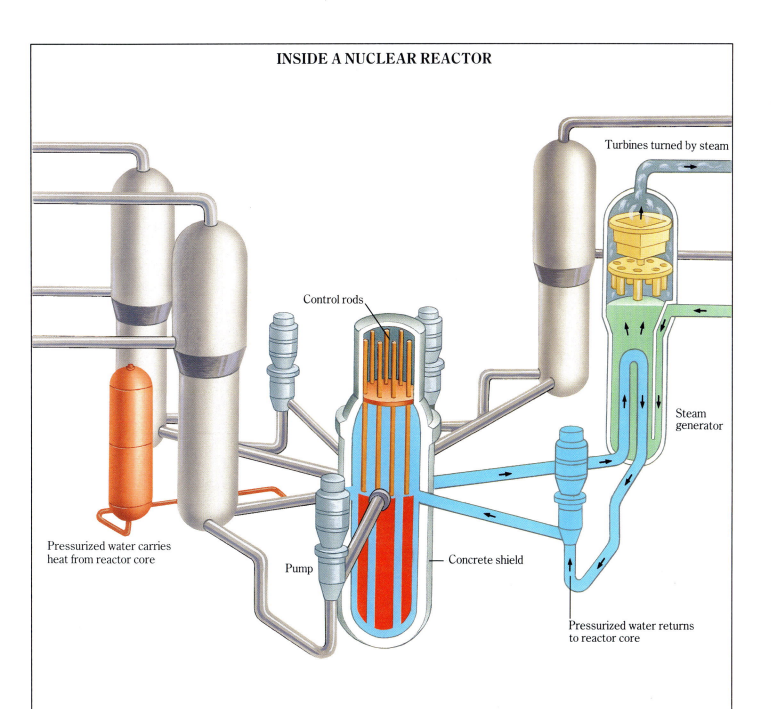

In a nuclear power station, the process of nuclear fission is carefully controlled. The uranium used gets very hot, and a **coolant** (a liquid or gas) moves through the reactor to be heated. When hot, the coolant goes to a boiler to make steam, which powers electric generators. In the reactor in the picture, water is used at high pressure as the coolant. In an advanced gas-cooled reactor, the gas carbon dioxide acts as the coolant throughout the reactor.

Inside the reactor core, uranium nuclei split as neutron particles strike them. The smaller nuclei, together with neutrons and invisible rays, called gamma rays, move off at great speed, producing heat.

Although nuclear reactors are a very efficient way of producing electricity, they produce large amounts of dangerous radioactive waste. Disposing of this waste safely is a very serious problem.

RADIOACTIVITY
This sign is used to warn of the presence of **radioactive** materials. Some waste from nuclear power stations is radioactive—it produces deadly nuclear radiation that can kill living cells.

HOW DO WE KNOW

What's the Attraction?

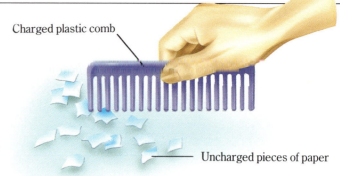

Charged plastic comb

Uncharged pieces of paper

Some materials can attract other materials to them. This results from one of two invisible forces: magnetism and static electricity.

Magnetism is the name given to the force with which a magnet attracts magnetic materials. Nobody knows for certain how magnets work. Scientists think that, in materials like iron and steel, each atom is a miniature magnet. Normally the atoms point in all directions, and their magnetic effects cancel each other. But when a material is magnetized, its atoms line up in the same direction, and it becomes one big magnet. An electric current flowing through a coil of wire produces a magnet, called an electromagnet, that can be switched on and off.

Static electricity consists of an electric charge that remains in one place rather than flowing around as an electric current. Static electricity was the first kind of electricity to be discovered. One effect of it is that when two materials are rubbed together, one of them may be attracted to a third kind of material.

MAKING STATIC ELECTRICITY

There are two types of electrical charges: positive and negative. Objects usually contain equal numbers of both charges, so that they cancel each other out.

Rub a plastic comb against a woolen sweater. The comb will pick up electrons from the wool. Electrons carry a negative charge. Now put the comb near some small pieces of uncharged paper. If the comb has a negative charge, it will repel the electrons on the paper nearest to it. This will leave the paper with a positive charge at one end, and it will be attracted to the comb and stick to it.

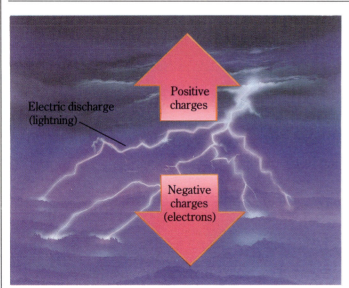

Electric discharge (lightning)

Positive charges

Negative charges (electrons)

HOW LIGHTNING IS PRODUCED

In very hot weather, clouds may become charged with static electricity when particles inside them rub against each other. Positive charges tend to collect at the top of the cloud, while negative charges move to the bottom. Eventually the charge builds up so much that the negative charges (the electrons) jump from one side of the cloud to the other as they try to "balance" themselves. When they jump, the surrounding air gets very hot. This is what causes the flash of lightning and also makes a shock wave of pressure that we hear as thunder.

Cloud-to-ground lightning
Sometimes a very big charge on a cloud can induce an opposite charge to build up on the earth below. An electric current then flows toward the earth in a jagged pattern called "forked" lightning. If the current hits anything, such as a tree, a building, or even a person, it burns it. That is why it is dangerous to seek shelter under a tree or to stand on high ground during a thunderstorm.

34

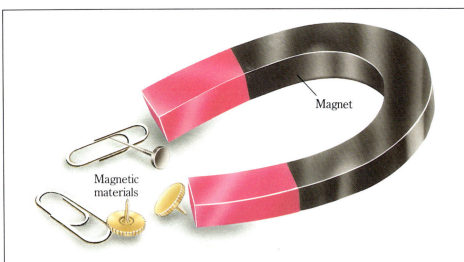

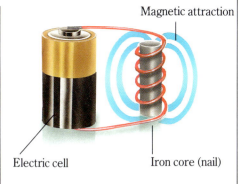

MAGNETIC ATTRACTION

Permanent magnets are usually made of iron, steel, cobalt, and nickel. Magnets can transfer their magnetism temporarily to other magnetic materials. In other words a magnet will attract objects made of, or that contain, iron, steel, cobalt, or nickel.

If we take a magnetic material, such as an iron nail, and stroke it evenly in the same direction a number of times with a magnet, the material will itself become a permanent magnet. The more it is stroked, the more powerful a magnet it will be. Hitting, dropping, or heating a magnet will jumble up its atoms and make it lose its magnetism.

HOW AN ELECTROMAGNET WORKS

An electromagnet is a kind of temporary magnet that can be switched on and off. It is made by winding insulated wire around an iron core. When an electric current is passed through the wire, it magnetizes the iron. The iron loses its magnetism when the current is switched off.

Magnetic poles
The forces from a magnet seem to come from its ends. These are called **poles**. One is north and the other south. If you have two magnets with the same poles facing each other, they push each other away. Opposite poles attract each other.

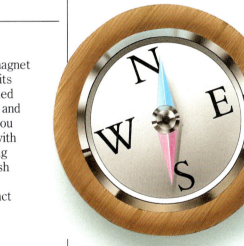

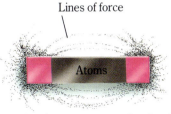

Magnetic fields
You cannot see what makes a magnet work, but it is possible to see the forces around a magnet. All magnets have what is called a magnetic field around them. You can "see" a magnetic field if you cover a magnet with a sheet of thin cardboard and sprinkle iron filings evenly on the cardboard. The iron filings arrange themselves in a pattern, which is the magnetic field. The lines are called lines of force. The lines of force are concentrated at the poles of the magnet, where its powers of attraction or repulsion are greatest.

COMPASSES

The needle inside a magnetic compass is a thin, light magnet that swings freely. The Earth has a magnetic field that extends from the poles all over the globe. It causes the needle of a magnetic compass to point toward the Earth's magnetic North Pole. People use magnetic compasses to find their way on land and at sea.

HOW DO WE KNOW

How Engines Work?

An engine is a machine that converts energy into mechanical energy, which is used to do work. In other words, engines can make things move. To do this, they burn fuel to produce heat. The heat makes gas or steam expand, and the force of expansion produces movement.

Engines can power anything from a lawn mower to a train or a space rocket. The world's most powerful engines are the rocket engines that lift a spacecraft into orbit.

The first engines used steam. You can easily see how steam exerts a force if you watch a pot of boiling water. The steam from the boiling water keeps lifting the lid. The first practical use of the steam engine was for pumping water out of mines. In 1698 the English engineer, Thomas Savery, invented a "fire engine" that pumped water. This was subsequently improved by later inventors.

The engines used today are called internal combustion engines. Aircraft, cars, trucks, buses, boats, and other forms of transportation burn fuel inside the engine, rather than outside as in a steam engine. The internal combustion engine is generally smaller, safer, and more powerful.

HOW A JET ENGINE WORKS

Basically, aircraft jet engines suck air in at one end of a tube and force it out the other end at a much greater speed. As a result the engine, and with it the aircraft, is thrust in the opposite direction.

To speed up the air passing through the tube, jet engines have powerful fans to suck in the incoming air. Some of this air is compressed and then mixed with fuel that is burned. The resulting gases expand suddenly and rush out of the back of the engine. This pushes the aircraft forward.

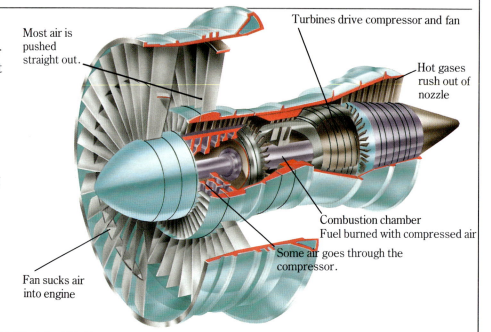

Most air is pushed straight out.
Turbines drive compressor and fan
Hot gases rush out of nozzle
Combustion chamber Fuel burned with compressed air
Some air goes through the compressor.
Fan sucks air into engine

1st stage

Nose section containing satellites
Fuel tanks
Engines

A ROCKET MOTOR

Fireworks and rockets that propel spacecraft into orbit work in basically the same way. They burn fuel quickly to produce large quantities of hot gases. These expand rapidly and rush out the back of the rocket pushing the rocket upward. However, while a firework rocket needs oxygen from air in order to burn, a space rocket can burn even in space where there is no air.

A space rocket motor overcomes the problems of the lack of air in space by carrying its own supply of liquid oxygen. The fuel is usually kerosene or liquid hydrogen. The oxygen is fed through a valve into the combustion chamber, where it is mixed with kerosene or liquid hydrogen. When the two are burned, they expand, producing a high-speed exhaust of very hot gases.

Three stages
To escape from the Earth, a rocket must travel at a speed of at least 17.5 miles (11 km) per second. A single craft could not carry enough fuel to reach this speed. It would be too heavy to leave the ground. So a spacecraft has separate

36

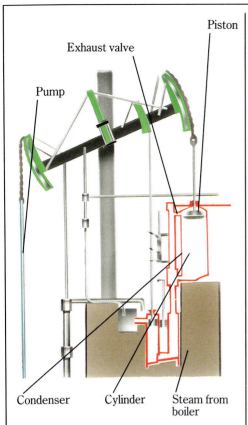

HOW A CAR ENGINE WORKS

A car engine creates the power that drives the car. The source of the engine's power is its pistons. The number of pistons in a car may vary from two up to twelve in a very large car.

Most cars have four-stroke engines—the piston goes through four up-and-down strokes. As the piston moves down, it draws in a mixture of fuel and air from the carburetor. Next the piston moves up, compressing the mixture (squeezing it into a smaller space). This compression makes it explode more efficiently in the next stroke, when a spark from the spark plug ignites the mixture. The explosion forces the piston down and turns the crankshaft, which powers the car's driving wheels. Finally, the exhaust stroke starts when the exhaust valve opens, the piston rises, and the burned gases are pushed out into the exhaust system.

JAMES WATT'S STEAM ENGINE

Most steam engines use coal or oil as their fuel. The heat from the burning fuel turns water into steam in a boiler. The steam is trapped under pressure in a metal cylinder. It expands and pushes a **piston** up and down in a cylinder. James Watt made a major breakthrough in steam engine design when, in 1765, he built an engine that had a separate condenser for cooling the steam.

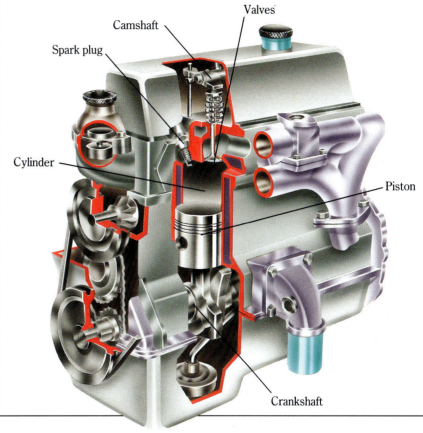

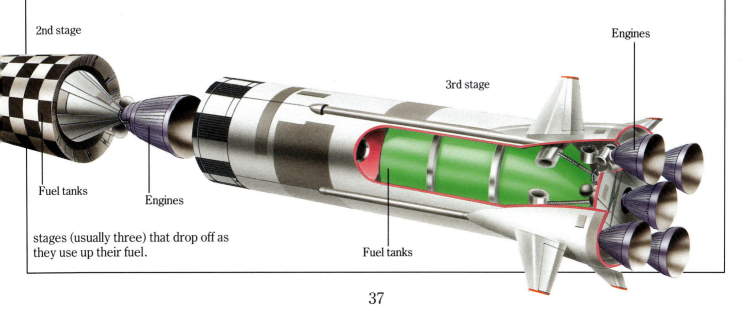

stages (usually three) that drop off as they use up their fuel.

HOW DO WE KNOW

How to Make Transportation Energy Efficient?

In the industrialized countries, people burn vast quantities of coal, oil, and gas. They use these fuels for heating and cooking, to power cars, and to manufacture all kinds of chemicals, including plastics, fertilizers, pesticides, drugs and medicines, and paint. Amazingly, about a quarter of all the fuels used in some industrialized countries are used in transportation.

The burning of fossil fuels in motor vehicles and aircraft is causing great damage to the environment. It releases gases, which are major causes of pollution and which may have harmful effects on the world climate, into the air.

If this was not a big enough problem, there is the added one that the world's supplies of fossil fuels will run out one day. And when they have run out, they can never be replaced. In the case of nonrenewable resources, such as coal, oil, and gas, the best we can do is to use them as carefully as possible.

Humans have always tried to find better ways of moving themselves and their goods around. But now the task is an urgent one. Scientists and engineers are striving to find more efficient forms of transportation and new sources of energy. They believe that the supplies of fossil fuels are more valuable for the production of important chemicals than for fueling cars, which can be done in alternative ways. As a result, in the future, most forms of land, sea, and air transportation are likely to be quieter, use less fuel, and cause less pollution.

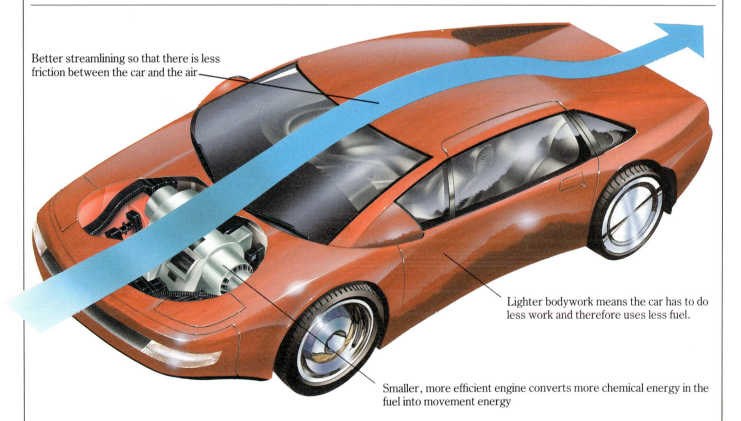

Better streamlining so that there is less friction between the car and the air

Lighter bodywork means the car has to do less work and therefore uses less fuel.

Smaller, more efficient engine converts more chemical energy in the fuel into movement energy

MORE EFFICIENT CARS
One way to make the existing supplies of fuel last longer is to use them more efficiently. The more easily a car slips through the air, the less fuel is needed to keep it moving. Lighter bodywork means that the car has to do less work. Finally, smaller, more efficient engines, which convert more of the chemical energy in gasoline into mechanical energy, will result in less fuel being used and less pollution. The "lean burn" engine developed by the Ford Motor Company has already cut gasoline consumption by 10 percent, as well as reducing harmful exhaust emissions.

38

BICYCLES

Make sure the seat is at the right height.

Keep the tires properly inflated.

Oil all moving parts.

One of the most environmentally friendly forms of transportation is the bicycle. When we ride a bicycle (as when we walk), we are using only muscle power. We are not using precious fossil fuels, nor are we causing noise or polluting the air.

There are ways of making bicycles more energy efficient, too. Make sure the bike is the right size for the rider, so the rider uses just the right amount of leg power. And inflate the tires properly. The less wheel on the ground, the less friction.

SOLAR-POWERED CARS

The sun's energy can be collected by special panels and used to make electricity to power small road vehicles and aircraft. In these machines, special cells are used to turn the sun's light energy into electricity. A single cell produces only a tiny amount of electricity, but a large number of cells connected together can make a useful amount of power.

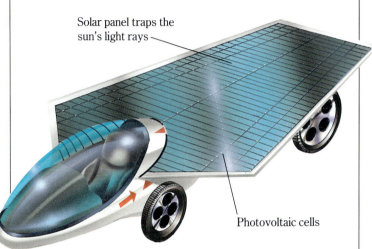

Solar panel traps the sun's light rays

Photovoltaic cells

RAILROAD TRAVEL

Most cars travel with only one or two people in them, whereas one bus can carry as many people as 40 cars can. Trains are an even more efficient method of transportation. They use much less fuel and produce much less pollution than the equivalent number of cars or trucks. Because of the damage road vehicles do to the environment, many people believe trains are the best type of transportation for the future.

For passengers, high-speed trains are a convenient way of traveling between large cities. Several countries have developed high-speed, long-distance trains. The French TGV trains for example (illustrated below) hold the world train speed record of 318 miles per hour (198 kph). An even newer and very fast type of intercity transportation is the Maglev train. This type of train floats above a special track on an invisible magnetic field.

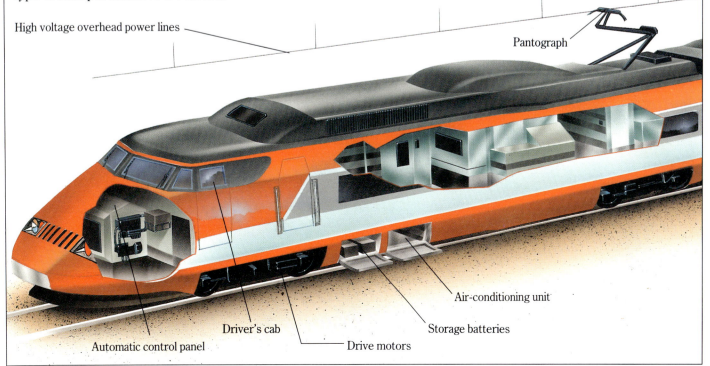

High voltage overhead power lines

Pantograph

Automatic control panel

Driver's cab

Drive motors

Storage batteries

Air-conditioning unit

39

Glossary

Aphids
Small insect pests that live on the leaves and shoots of plants. They feed on plant juices

Atom
The smallest particle of a chemical element that can exist and have all the properties of that element. All the matter in the universe is made up of atoms.

Chemicals
Substances—elements or compounds—that have characteristic molecular compositions

Chlorophyll
The substance that gives plants their green color

Convection currents
Currents caused by the movement of heat from one place to another in a liquid or gas

Coolant
A liquid or gas used to remove heat from an engine or a nuclear reactor

Deposits
Materials that are laid down or left behind by water or the wind

Electrodes
Conductors through which an electric current enters or leaves a battery or some other electrical device

Electrons
Tiny particles of matter that orbit around the nucleus of an atom. An electron has a negative electric charge.

Gear wheel
A toothed wheel that transfers movement from one part of a machine to another

Generators
Machines that change mechanical energy into electrical energy

Geyser
A natural spring that sends a blast of hot water or steam into the air

Gravity
The invisible pull on all objects due to the Earth, moon, or other bodies in space. Gravity attracts smaller objects on or near the Earth's surface toward the center of the Earth.

Lubricants
Slippery substances, such as oil or grease, used to coat the moving parts of machinery, so that they move smoothly against each other, reducing friction and wear

Molecule
The smallest particle of a substance that can exist and still have the properties of the substance

Phosphor
A substance that glows when excited by radiation

Piston
A circular disk or cylindrical piece of metal that moves up and down inside a tightly fitting cylinder

Poles
The ends of a magnet where the magnetic force is greatest; also the north and south ends of the Earth's axis

Radioactive
Giving off harmful radiation in the form of tiny particles or waves

Reactions
The process in which two or more substances have an effect on each other and new substances are produced

Shaft
A metal bar that passes on movement from one part of an engine to another; also a long, narrow space going straight up and down, for example, in a mine

Sonar machine
A device that uses the echoes created by pulses of sound hitting objects to locate submarines, wrecks, or schools of fish, or to measure the depth of the ocean

Starch
A white, powdery substance with no taste or smell that occurs in potatoes, rice, corn, root crops, and many other plants. Starch is used as a food.

Streamlining
The designing and building of an aircraft, ship, car, or some other object so that it moves smoothly through air or water

Swamps
Marshes or other areas of very wet, soft ground that have trees growing on them

Transparent
Describes any material that lets light through, so that things are clearly seen on the other side

Turbine
A wheel with blades turned by water, steam, or the wind

Valve
A device for controlling the flow of liquids or gases through an opening or along a pipe

Index

A
air resistance 15
aircraft 5, 15, 18, 35
animals 20, 22, 23, 24
argon gas 28
atoms 32

B
batteries 30–31
bicycles 14, 15, 39
brakes 14
bulldozers 5

C
carbohydrates 22
carbon dioxide 9, 11
cars 11, 14, 17, 30, 37
    energy efficient 38, 39
cells, electric 30, 31
chemical energy 7, 8, 10, 11, 22, 23
chlorophyll 9
circuits, electrical 28–29
clocks 12
coal 24, 25, 37, 38
compasses, magnetic 35
conduction
    electricity 28
    heat 16
convection, heat 16, 26

D
dams 12
digestive system 23

E
ears 18
echoes 19
electrical energy 7, 9, 10, 11, 12, 28–29
    generating 25, 26–27
    static electricity 34
    "waste" of 17
electrodes 29
electromagnetism 20, 34, 35
electrons 28, 32, 34
engines 5, 11, 17, 36–38
experiments
    chemical energy 11
    conductors 16
    friction 14
    insulators 16
    sound vibrations 19
    static electricity 34
    sun's energy 8
eyes 21

F
fats 22
fireflies 20
fireworks 11, 36
flashlights 30–31
fluorescent light bulbs 29
food 7, 8, 9, 10, 12, 22–23
food chain 23
fossil fuels 24–25, 38, 39
friction 14–15
fuels 5, 12, 17, 24–25, 36, 37, 38
fuses, electrical 29

G
gamma rays 33
gas 25, 38
generators 12, 25, 26–27, 33
geothermal energy 9
geysers 9
glowworms 20
greenhouse 9, 21

H
heat 6, 8–9, 10, 11, 28–29
    transfer 16–17
heater, electric 29
helium 32
home insulation 17
hydraulic rams 27
hydroelectricity 12
hydrogen 32, 36

I
ice 16
infrared rays 6, 8, 20, 21
insulators 16, 17
    of electricity 28
internal combustion engines 17, 36–37

J
jet engines 36

K
kerosene 36
kinetic energy 6, 7, 10, 11, 12, 13, 26

L
lasers 20
light 6, 8, 10, 11, 20–21
    light bulbs 17, 28, 29
lightning 34
lubricants 14

M
Maglev train 39
magnetic energy 7, 31, 34–35
mechanical energy 6, 17, 31
microphones 11
microwaves 20
minerals 22
mining 24
molecules 6, 16, 18, 32
moon 20, 26
motorcycles 5
motors, electric 31
musical instruments 5

N
neutrons 32
nitrogen gas 28
nuclear energy 7, 10, 32–33

O
oil 24, 25, 37, 38
oscilloscopes 19

P
peat 24
phosphor 29
photosynthesis 9
pile drivers 13
planets 20
plants 8, 9, 22, 23, 24, 25
pollution 38
porcelain 29
potential energy 12
power stations 25, 33
proteins 22
protons 32

R
radiation, heat 16
radio 10, 18, 20
radioactivity 33
railroads 39
rain 26
rainbows 20
reactors, nuclear 33
resistance, electrical 28, 29
rocket motors 36–37

S
Savery, Thomas 36
shadows 21
skates 15
sledding 15
solar system 8
solar-powered cars 39
sonar machines 19
sound 6, 10, 11, 18–19
spacecraft 36–37
sports 4, 10
starch 9, 22
static electricity 34
steam power 36, 37
storing energy 12–13
streamlining 15
sun 6, 8, 16, 20, 21
    nuclear energy 32
    water cycle 26
switches, electrical 28, 29

T
television 11, 20
TGV trains 39
thunder 34
tidal power 26, 27
trains 39
tungsten 28
tuning forks 18
turbines 12, 25, 26, 27, 33, 36

U
ultraviolet rays 6, 8, 20, 29
uranium 32, 33

V
vitamins 22
Volta, Alessandro 30

W
watches 12
water 16
    water cycle 26
Watt, James 37
wave power 26, 27
weight lifting 10
wind power 7, 26, 27
windmill 7

X
X rays 6, 20

© Simon & Schuster
Young Books, 1993